I am a fifty-two-year-old, French, woman author. I like the English language. I was born in Mauritius, and I live in Reunion Island. My Mauritius Island has a special place in my heart, and it will remain forever. I owe who I am to my mum. I close this book by dedicating my words to her.

This is a work of fiction. Names, characters, businesses, places, events and incidents are either the product of the author's imagination or used in a fictitious manner. Any resemblance to actual persons, living or dead, or actual events is purely coincidental.

Geneviève Langlois

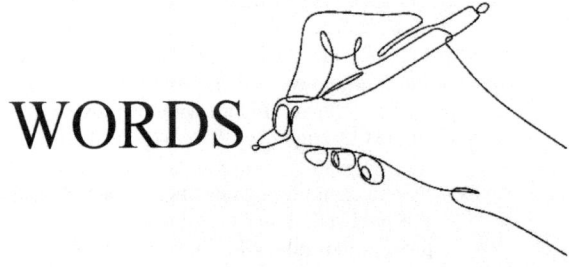
WORDS

Vanguard Press

VANGUARD PAPERBACK

© Copyright 2024

Geneviève Langlois

The right of Geneviève Langlois to be identified as author of
this work has been asserted by her in accordance with the
Copyright, Designs and Patents Act 1988.

All Rights Reserved

No reproduction, copy or transmission of this publication
may be made without written permission.
No paragraph of this publication may be reproduced,
copied or transmitted save with the written permission of the
publisher, or in accordance with the provisions
of the Copyright Act 1956 (as amended).

Any person who commits any unauthorised act in relation to
this publication may be liable to criminal
prosecution and civil claims for damages.

A CIP catalogue record for this title is
available from the British Library.

ISBN 978 1 837947 078 3

*Vanguard Press is an imprint of
Pegasus Elliot Mackenzie Publishers Ltd.*
www.pegasuspublishers.com

First Published in 2024

**Vanguard Press
Sheraton House Castle Park
Cambridge England**

Printed & Bound in Great Britain

To my mum, with all my love, forever.

To my mum who always believed in me.
For my both parents that have gone.
Love you both.

Contents

Winter is Coming	11
Let's go to London	12
Good Trip in the Bus	13
The British Weather	14
A Bee	15
In the Big Wheel	16
To My Friend	17
My Garden	18
Oh! Happily in London	19
Spread the Bread	20
In Silence	21
The Rain	22
Holiday	23
In a Beautiful Town like London	24
Easter is Near!	25
In Winter, in London —We Were Out There!	26
Peace In This World	27
The Key of Success	28
August is There!	29
Stop Racism	30
Halloween	31
Time of Hope, Time of Wishes	32
Christmas	33
New Year is Coming	34
The Cyclone is Coming	35
Cyclone Season	36
Peace Starts in Your Heart	37
Kindness	38
Goodbye, April. Goodbye, my April Mum	39
Last thoughts. Last Poem is for You, My Darling Mum.	40

Winter is Coming

Oh, oh! Winter is coming!
Come and enjoy!
Look outside! it has started snowing! Which coat to wear,
 I am wondering! Oh, oh! Winter is coming!
Santa Claus is preparing! Christmas will be singing!
Everywhere in the town, joy it will bring.
Oh, oh! Winter is coming!
Church's bells will ring!

Let's go to London

Going to London on the ferry. I agree; going to London on the Thames, I'm happy.

Going to London by the road, it's funny. Going to London on the plane, with a cup of tea. Going to London by the tube and having a coffee. Let's go to London in December when it's snowy. Let's go to London in summer, when it's sunny. Let's go to London in autumn, when it's foggy. Let's go, let's go pick up flowers when it's spring.

Let's go, let's go together; it's more friendly.

Good Trip in the Bus

In the big bus — it's a must! Come on! Visit London with us.
Be kind, offer us a ticket for this bus! No need to argue, no need to discuss.
A pack of nuts, an ice-cream in the cup. Better guys than in your truck!
At ease. Just admire the landscape from the bus. In the pond — the ducks.
A bit further, some birds — can you trust? It's summer. Have a good trip in the bus.

The British Weather

Oh, London and its legendary fog! Grey outside, often rain and rain.

However, work inside or outside, with no pain. Wake up early in the morning again and again. Usual ways of living in this charming town remain.

An unforgettable city for everyone. Love what is offered, what is contained.

Beautiful London; drinking champagne in a cute and tiny cottage.

One day, take a time, and go to London by train. It will be great, but I will choose the plane!

A Bee

A bee in the garden, in the tree. Do you hear his song already?

A bee on the flower, near my cup of tea. Do you see he is not far from me?

A bee, near its hive, flies gently. Be careful — don't kill a bee.

A bee has an important role on Earth. Let him free.

In the Big Wheel

Climbing in the Big Wheel in London during summer —
    it's chilly.
Watching the landscape from the top of a hill.
Hurry up! Ask Mum and Dad for a round in the wheel.
    Holidays are here; the marinated meat will be on the
    grill. Laugh, joy and pleasure are real — can you feel?
Spending these moments together, we will ride on the Big
    Wheel and end with a great family meal. Smells good.
    Feel!

To My Friend

We all have a nice friend —someone who is so gentle to recommend.

A guy that you will love to the end. A person that you will always defend. With him, you will attend special occasions. Feelings, tenderness and joy you will experience together.

A friend for life to hold your hand. A good friend.

My Garden

In my garden in the summer, there are many colours and a good smell.
Flowers, trees and fruits, watered by Angel Grandfather, are doing a beautiful "aquarelle".
Happiness is in the air. We can hear the church's bell. Tom is playing on the beach with a shell.
In summer, in my garden, life is sweet, I can tell!

Oh! Happily in London

Spending summer alone?
Oh no! Together with John, Don and Simon!
Having one tasty scone and walking upon the bridge.
Drinking an English Tea with Dom. Oh! What a nice journey in London.

Spread the Bread

Spread the bread to the birds, said the baker.
Feed them with your heart. They are singing; can you hear?
The blue bird, the little, brown bird and the red bird. Cui! Cui! Cui! Cui! sings the little yellow bird.
Spread, spread.

In Silence

When you listen to the silence, everything becomes evidence. A single word can be an offense.
Waiting for someone, needing his presence.
Just appreciate the moment with patience. Give a break to the opulence.
Keep contact with the nature in silence. Improve your existence.

In a Beautiful Town like London

In a beautiful town like London, don't stay on your own. Enjoy moments with friends. London will make you grow. In the city, there are attractions. You can even meet a clown. Don't let problems put you down.
Come to London, even if there you are an unknown.

Easter is Near!

Rabbits are ready — can you see them here?
Oh, yes! A hen and her little chicks have just appeared.
 Candies and mostly chocolate bears.
Kids will have choice dear.
The chime of the Easter bells will be heard. Easter songs
 will bring joy just near.
Let the happiness of the egg hunt come here.
Happy Easter to you, dear.

In Winter, in London — We Were Out There!

On that road together, and guess where?
In the bus, in the cab, in the tube and elsewhere.
We were there night and day — lovely air. Appreciate the moment in the theatre. Eating English pudding at the baker. Enjoy the city and its events offered.
Sitting there, reading books of a great writer.
London will make you happier.

Peace in this World

Bring peace, joy, love and happiness in this world. Pray, sing and live in serenity.

Share, offer and give love all around this world. Peacefulness start at home.

Spread it around the world. This is how love will overcome hate.

Make love in your world.

The Key of Success

Back to school.
Happiness to be among our friends, respect the coat dress. Ready for good marks and guess.
No way to transgress, we need to be the best.
Respect everyone, forget the mess. Let's perform and impress.
We are ready to study, ready and free. Our destiny is in our hands, it's time to be.

August is There!

It is winter somewhere, while it is summer elsewhere. No leaves on the trees or lot of flowers everywhere.
Nature is doing her job, and when you observe, you can say how great is this affair.
Each step has his existing reason there.
Sun on the skin, rain on the head or wind in the hair. You can choose — it is a free offer forever.
The nature is generous — respect and share.

Stop Racism

Black lives matter.
First of all, we are citizens of the world, with the same blood colour.
When the time comes, we will leave.
At that time, we will all be in the same situation. Our colour will be of no importance any more.
Where we will go, all colours will be bright with beauty.
Think before criticizing colours of skin.
Love all, because love will always be stronger than war.
Love will put on its most beautiful colours.
Our colours.

Halloween

Halloween is here! Wear your terror clothes, dear!
Make your neighbours feel a bit of fear. Young children scared, please don't bring tears. Celebrate it with fun, to have a good souvenir.
Halloween is here! Pumpkins everywhere and near.
Happy Halloween, dear.

Time of Hope, Time of Wishes

Wonderful days will come pretty soon. Grandma will prepare the meal.

Uncle and Aunt will come with kisses, and Mum will decorate the house.

The gardener will cut the bushes, and Dad will install the Christmas tree.

After the lunch, children will wash the dishes. Grandad will install the Christmas crib. Everyone will sing and spread wishes.

Christmas

Here or there, it's Christmas everywhere. Everyone is quite busy to prepare.
People won't count the time, they'll care. Joy, laughter and love are in the air.
Please all by a simple care, Christmas is everywhere.
Magic to repair your soul, share and enjoy like a prayer.
Where? Where? Here and there, Christmas is everywhere.

New Year is Coming

Resolutions will be taking place. Hope that it will bring joy.
New start, new project; give us wings. Stop complaining.
Stop saying bad things. Stop smoking.
Be better with others and in everything. Enjoy life by loving.
Happy New Year, darling!

The Cyclone is Coming

It's raining outside, the wind is blowing. Stay inside, while this weather is spoiling.
Enjoy a meal, or if you prefer, choose reading. A good book — a novel — may be interesting.
Lots of ideas can cross your mind while sleeping — writing, drawing, painting and music-playing.
Take care and stay safe — the cyclone is coming.

Cyclone Season

Everyone is inside. The TV is on, the food is ready, and the dessert is done. The wind will blow strongly upon.
Close windows and doors without forgetting any. Stay inside, the weather forecast will give the tone.
Charge your phone.
Tomorrow this cyclone will be on. For the moment, the priority is to relax. Keep the news on.

Peace Starts in Your Heart

Peace starts in your heart. Peace begins in our house. Peace lives inside your soul.

Peace is when you smile at your neighbours. Peace is when you help the elders. Peace is when you listen to others. Peace is everywhere when you decide.

Spread your town and your country with peace.

Kindness

Be kind with the one who gave you education. Be respectful in your communication.
Never speak loudly, preserve your relation. Parents are there and need your participation.
Even if you faced separation, you have their admiration. They offered you the best attention.
Now they are old, treat them with love and compassion. One day you will suffer of their disparition.

Goodbye, April. Goodbye, my April Mum

You will come back next year with your flowers. Goodbye, April.
We wished happy birthday to Mum, Bill, Gill and Phil. Goodbye, April.
Take with you this war; pray for people that were killed. Goodbye, April.
Leave some energy in the air; we may have to climb the hills. Goodbye, April.

Last thoughts.
Last Poem is for You,
My Darling Mum.

I thought of you, you are so far away. Maybe at that time, you are sitting down on a cloud.
Watching me and protecting me.
Maybe you are busy walking in a blossom garden.
Maybe you are reading my poems.
Maybe you are resting by, keeping an eye on my writing. Maybe you are laughing at what I wrote.
Birds, London, cyclone, Winter, Halloween, April, bee, garden and more.
Maybe you are flying next to this bird around me. Maybe you are this butterfly that has just landed down next to me.
Or you are this blowing wind that caresses my neck. You are everywhere, because I am keeping you in me as a treasure, my mum.
I am sure you are there somewhere.
I love you forever, Mum.